Understanding People In The Past
The ANCIENT ROMANS

ROSEMARY REES

Heinemann
LIBRARY

www.heinemann.co.uk/library
Visit our website to find out more information about **Heinemann Library** books.

To order:
☎ Phone ++44 (0)1865 888066
🖹 Send a fax to ++44 (0)1865 314091
🖥 Visit the Heinemann Bookshop at www.heinemann.co.uk/library to browse our catalogue and order online.

First published in Great Britain by Heinemann Library, Halley Court, Jordan Hill, Oxford OX2 8EJ, part of Harcourt Education.
Heinemann is a registered trademark of Harcourt Education Ltd.

Editorial: Clare Lewis
Design: Michelle Lisseter and Damco Solutions Ltd
Picture research: Hannah Taylor
Production: Helen McCreath

Originated by Dot Gradations Ltd
Printed and bound in China by WKT Company Ltd

10-digit ISBN: 0 431 07794 0
13-digit ISBN: 978 0 431 07794 9
10 09 08 07 06
10 9 8 7 6 5 4 3 2 1

British Library Cataloging in Publication Data
Rees, Rosemary, 1942-
    The ancient Romans. - 2nd ed. - (Understanding People in the Past)
    937'.06
    A full catalogue record for this book is available from the British Library.

Acknowledgments
The author and publisher are grateful to the following for permission to reproduce copyright material:
R. Agache, p. 24; Ancient Art and Architecture Collection, pp. 5 top, 6 top, 8 left and right, 9 top, 12 bottom, 13, 14 bottom, 19, 21, 22 top, 23 top, 30, 33 right, 35 top, 38 left, 40, 42, 45 top and bottom, 49, 50 right, 51, 52 bottom, 55, 56 top, 59; British Museum, p. 16 left; C.M. Dixon, pp. 5 bottom, 10, 26 top, 31 left, 35 bottom; Sonia Halliday Photographs, pp. 6 bottom, 38 right; Michael Holford, title page, pp. 7, 14 top, 15, 16 top, 23 bottom, 31 right and left, 36, 39, 41, 43 top and bottom, 46, 47, 54, 56 bottom, 57, 58; Hulton Picture Company, p 52 top; Museum of London/Jan Sorivener, pp. 9 bottom, 34; Mansell Collection, pp. 12 top, 17, 20, 50 left; Picturepoint, p. 28; Scala, p. 18; Trustees of the National Museums of Scotland, p. 27; Reg Wilson, p. 53.
Cover photograph © The Art Archive / Provincial Museum GM Kam, Mijmegen, Netherlands / Dagli Orti.

The publishers would like to thank Dr. Michael Vickers for his advice on the content of this book.

Every effort has been made to contact copyright holders of any material reproduced in this book. Any omissions will be rectified in subsequent printings if notice is given to the publisher.

Some words are shown in bold, **like this**. You can find out what they mean by looking in the glossary.

CONTENTS

WHO WERE THE ROMANS?

Between 2000 and 1000 BC, people from central Asia began moving into the country we now call Italy. One group settled by the Tiber River. The people farmed the flat land by the river and traded with other settlers. They built villages on the seven hilltops surrounding their settlement. These villages became the city of Rome.

Kings

The Romans chose their kings. Lucius Tarquinius was the seventh and last king of Rome. He was cruel and unpopular. In 510 BC, the Romans drove him out.

BC and AD

Each year has a number. These numbers, or dates, count the years before and after the year Jesus Christ was born. Dates before the birth of Christ have the letters BC written after them, for example, 2000 BC. BC stands for "before Christ". Remember that 1000 BC is closer in time to us than 2000 BC. Dates after the birth of Christ have the letters AD written in front of them, for example, AD 900. AD stands for *Anno Domini*. These words mean "in the year of our Lord" in the Latin language. The Romans divided their year into months to match changes in the moon.

Their year had 355 days, and the months slowly got out of step with the seasons. Julius Caesar started a new calendar. It had 365 days like the calendar used today.

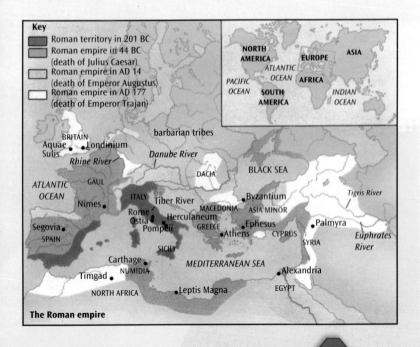

Key
- Roman territory in 201 BC
- Roman empire in 44 BC (death of Julius Caesar)
- Roman empire in AD 14 (death of Emperor Augustus)
- Roman empire in AD 177 (death of Emperor Trajan)

NORTH AMERICA · EUROPE · ASIA
ATLANTIC OCEAN · AFRICA
PACIFIC OCEAN · SOUTH AMERICA · INDIAN OCEAN

BRITAIN · Aquae Sulis · Londinium · barbarian tribes · Rhine River · Danube River · DACIA · BLACK SEA · ATLANTIC OCEAN · GAUL · Nimes · ITALY · Tiber River · Byzantium · Tigris River · Rome · Ostia · Herculaneum · MACEDONIA · ASIA MINOR · Pompeii · GREECE · Ephesus · Palmyra · Segovia · Athens · CYPRUS · SYRIA · Euphrates River · SPAIN · SICILY · Carthage · MEDITERRANEAN SEA · Alexandria · Timgad · NUMIDIA · Leptis Magna · EGYPT · NORTH AFRICA

The Roman empire

Roman roads, bridges, and buildings can still be seen today. The Colosseum in Rome was finished in AD 80. It is 52 metres (170 feet) high and once held 50,000 people.

The republic

The Romans set up a **republic** in 509 BC. They still chose their leader, but only for a fixed time. Then they chose a new one. Rome was a republic for 500 years. The Romans became powerful and conquered other lands, including Greece.

The empire

In 27 BC, the Romans made Augustus their first **emperor**. He ruled over Rome and all the lands conquered by the Romans. He was the ruler of more than 60 million people.

For 300 years, the Romans spread their skills and knowledge throughout their **empire**.

This wall painting is from a house in the town of Pompeii. It is about 2,000 years old. Experts think it is a picture of the owner of the house and his wife.

HOW DO WE KNOW ABOUT THE ROMANS?

Archaeologists have uncovered clues about the Romans. They dig in the ground and **excavate** buried objects. They find pottery, jewellery, and household objects. These objects give clues about how the Romans lived. They also find graves. Objects buried with the dead tell us about their religious beliefs. Sometimes archaeologists uncover entire buildings, towns, and cities.

In AD 79, the volcano Vesuvius erupted. Hot ash and mud buried the cities of Herculaneum and Pompeii. These two cities were found accidentally.

Archaeologists carefully uncover everything they find.

Some ancient Roman buildings can still be seen. This is Palmyra in the desert of Syria, in the Middle East.

In 1709, men digging a well found the Herculaneum **amphitheatre**. Years later, a farmer who was ploughing fields found the city of Pompeii.

In AD 365, Ammianus Marcellinus saw and wrote about an earthquake on Cyprus. Archaeologists followed the ancient written clues. In the 1970s, they found the Roman town of Kourion on Cyprus. It was the town that had been buried by that earthquake.

Legend or fact?

A Roman legend tells how Rome began. Romulus and Remus were twin brothers. Their wicked uncle threw the babies into the Tiber River. But they didn't drown. A she-wolf heard them crying. She looked after them until a shepherd found them. He and his wife raised the boys as if they were their own children.

When the twins grew up, they decided to build a city at the place where they were rescued. They began to build the city. But they quarrelled, and Romulus killed Remus. The city of Rome, begun in 753 BC, is named after Romulus, its first king.

EVIDENCE IN WORDS AND PICTURES

Books and letters

The Romans wrote books about their past. Livy, an historian, wrote 142 books on Roman history. The Romans wrote letters about their daily lives. Pliny the Younger wrote hundreds of letters to his friends. His letters tell about Roman life from AD 55 to 120.

Words on walls

Archaeologists found graffiti on walls in Pompeii. People wrote on walls then, just as they do today. Some graffiti said things about elections of town officials. "Vote for Julius Philippus and he'll do the same for you" was one slogan uncovered by archaeologists.

Sometimes the Romans wrote on papyrus. This is a type of paper made from reeds. Writing carved into stone can still be read today. Words on a tombstone, like this one, often praise the dead person.

Latin

Latin was the official language of the Roman Empire. The conquered countries of the empire were expected to speak and read Latin. Latin still exists because it was the language of the Catholic Church. Church services were conducted in Latin.

Words and images that last

Archaeologists have found important documents and certificates written on bronze. Bronze is a long-lasting metal.

Wall paintings also tell us much about everyday Roman life. Statues, sculptures, and carvings show how people looked.

This stone carving shows Roman clothes and hairstyles. A lady is having her hair done. Her maids are helping her.

*Archaeologists have uncovered **mosaic** floors. The Romans made mosaics from small tiles of coloured stone or pottery. When they laid the floors, they made pictures of Roman life using the coloured stone.*

GOVERNMENT

When Rome became a republic in 509 BC, the people were determined that no one person should have too much power.

The **citizens** of Rome met in four groups called comitia. Every year each of the comitia elected **magistrates**. Their names were written on a board in the **forum**, which was the central meeting place in Rome. Magistrates had the power to enforce the law. The most powerful magistrates were the two **consuls**. They had to agree with each other because one consul could cancel, or veto, the other's decisions.

Women, slaves, and people not born in Rome were not citizens. This meant they could not vote to choose their leaders.

The Forum Romanum was the centre of religion. These remaining columns were part of the Temple of Castor and Pollux. Romans believed these gods helped them in battle.

The Forum Romanum

basilica Aemilia

basilica of Maxentius

temple

temple

temple

rostra

senate house or curia

Most magistrates also served as a member of the **Senate** for the rest of their lives. At different times, there were between 300 and 900 senators. They advised the consuls. After 27 BC, the Romans had an emperor. He chose the members of the Senate. He decided who would be the next emperor.

Each Roman territory, or **province**, was ruled by a governor. He ruled in the name of the people of Rome. The Senate, and later the emperor, chose the governors. They had usually served as magistrates in Rome.

The forum was an open market square, or meeting place. The Romans erected buildings around each side of the square. The Forum Romanum became the centre of government. The first curia, or Senate house, was built in 670 BC. This was where senators met to discuss problems. The basilicas were large halls used for banquets and as law courts. Politicians spoke to the people from the rostra.

PEOPLE AND THE LAW

Romans divided their citizens into two classes. **Patricians** were rich **nobles** who owned a lot of land. **Plebeians** were tradesmen, servants, and men with small farms. The patricians had more votes than the plebeians. Only patricians could become magistrates and senators.

By 494 BC, the plebeians had had enough of this inequality. They threatened to leave Rome. The patricians agreed that the plebeians could choose two officers called **tribunes**. The tribunes had the power to veto actions of the magistrates or consuls. After 366 BC, one consul was always a plebeian.

Slaves worked for nothing and were often badly treated by their owners. Many slaves worked in mines or on farms. The life of a household slave was easier. Slaves had no legal rights and could not vote. Slaves could be freed when their masters died.

This writing is a political advertisement for public fights put on by Lucretius Satrus. He hoped that this entertainment would persuade people to vote for Quintus Postumus.

Roman law

Roman law began in the families. These rules were handed down from one family to another. Then kings made rules and passed judgements. When the Roman Republic began in 509 BC, laws were not written. They were only spoken.

In 450 BC, the laws of Rome were written on bronze tablets. Punishments were written there, too. They were displayed in the forum for everyone to see.

Over hundreds of years, new laws were made. In AD 529, the Emperor Justinian ordered all the laws to be written in a Code of Law. Today, many countries base their laws on the laws of ancient Rome.

Cicero

Marcus Tullius Cicero lived from 106 BC to 43 BC. By 70 BC, he was Rome's most important lawyer. He became a consul in 63 BC. Cicero wrote many speeches and letters about the people and politics of Rome. More than 900 of his letters have survived. He translated the work of Greek philosophers and he wrote books of his own. Many of his ideas came from the Greeks. His writings were used as textbooks in schools. Teachers of public speaking gave Cicero's speeches to pupils as examples to follow.

WHAT DID ROMANS WEAR?

Most people's clothes were made from wool. Wealthy people had clothes made from linen and silk.

Men's clothes

Men wore a knee-length tunic with short sleeves and a belt. Roman citizens wore a **toga** over their tunics. A toga was like a long sheet that they wound around their bodies, over the left shoulder, and under the right arm.

Women's clothes

Women wore a long tunic with another tunic, called a **stola**, on top. When they went out, they wore a cloak, called a palla.

Archaeologists found necklaces, gold rings, and hairpins. Gold came from Spain. Jewels came from Asia. Children wore amulets, small carved charms, or lockets. Parents believed amulets would keep children safe.

Statues tell us a lot about Roman clothes. Men wore brooches to keep their togas in place. Men and women wore sandals at home and soft boots when they went out. Poor people and slaves went barefoot.

Children's clothes

Boys wore a short tunic with a cloak. Girls wore an ankle-length tunic with a shawl or cloak.

Hairstyles

Wealthy women had very fancy hairstyles. Their slaves styled their hair for them. Some women dyed their hair blonde. They bought blonde wigs and hairpieces. This is a Roman painting of a wealthy woman. She has an elaborate hairstyle. Her earrings and necklaces are made from gold and precious stones.

Men's hairstyles often followed that of the emperor. When the Emperor Hadrian grew a beard, hundreds of Roman men grew beards, too.

FAMILY LIFE

A Roman family, or familia, was more than just the father, mother, and children. It included slaves, servants, grandparents, unmarried aunts and uncles, and the **household gods**. The father was the head of the family.

Weddings

Fathers arranged marriages for their children. Girls married when they were about 13. Boys married when they were a little older. The fathers signed a marriage contract at the bride's home. There were prayers and a special cake was offered to the gods and goddesses.

This gold wedding ring shows clasped hands. The carving above shows a wedding ceremony. The bride and groom hold hands. The bride says, "Where you are master, I am mistress."

Then the bride went in a torchlight procession to the groom's house. He carried her through the doorway because if she tripped, there would be bad luck. Roman women kept their own property, but they were supposed to obey their husbands. A couple could divorce if they did not want to live together any more.

Roman names

When a baby was a few days old, it was shown to the father. If the father took the baby in his arms, the child was named and given a locket called a bulla. A baby had three names. The first was its own name, for example, Julia. The second was the name of the **clan**, for example, Tullius, and the third was the name of the family itself, for example, Cicero.

This carving shows a father and his son. First, the father watches his son as a baby being fed and then holds him. As a little boy, the son plays with a toy cart pulled by a goat. Children also played with hoops, dice, and dolls.

GOING TO SCHOOL

Children learned important things at home. Their parents taught them to obey rules, to tell the truth, and to help other people. When their parents had visitors, children stayed up late to listen to adult conversation. Cato wrote a book about how he taught his son at home.

Children could go to school when they were seven. They learned to read and write in Latin and Greek. They wrote with a pointed stick called a **stylus**. They did maths problems using beads on a frame called an **abacus**.

This girl is writing on a wooden board covered in wax. She is using a stylus. Sometimes girls from wealthy families stayed at school after they turned 13.

Most girls left school when they were 13. Boys went on to a grammaticus. There they learned about public speaking. They read Greek and Roman literature. Slaves made their books. The slaves copied the poems of Homer and Virgil on sheets of papyrus. These sheets were then glued together and rolled up into books.

Boys left school when they were 16. After school, boys from wealthy families could go to Athens in Greece. There they studied with the Greek **philosophers** or learned to become lawyers. Boys from poor families became **apprentices** and learned a trade or craft.

When a boy's first beard grew, he went through a special ceremony to show he was now a man. He put his toys away and was allowed to wear a toga.

Roman numerals

The Romans used letters for numbers, for example:

I = 1	V = 5
X = 10	L = 50
C = 100	D = 500
M = 1,000	

The numbers between are written as a series of letters before or after the main number.

4 = IV	6 = VI
15 = XV	56 = LVI

MMIX = 2009

GODS AND GODDESSES

The Romans believed in many gods and goddesses. They believed that if they pleased the gods, the gods would give them good luck. Romans thought that when they died, the god Mercury led their spirits into the **underworld** where gods and goddesses ruled.

The Romans worshipped the gods of the people that they conquered. They worshipped the gods of the Greeks. They worshipped Mithras from Persia, who gave courage and Isis from Egypt, who promised life after death. The Romans followed many different religions and cults. But in Britain, where **druid priests sacrificed** people and animals, Romans were not allowed to become druids.

*This tomb carving shows a procession of mourners. They are taking their loved one who has died to a burial ground. Sometimes the dead were buried or **cremated** with their belongings. Families remembered their dead at special yearly festivals.*

When the emperor Augustus died, the Roman Senate said he had become a god. Christians refused to worship the emperors. So the Romans persecuted them. The Romans killed thousands of Christians for their beliefs. Then, 300 years after the death of Jesus Christ, Emperor Constantine made Christianity the official religion of the Roman Empire.

The gods on this carving are, from left to right, Hercules, Minerva, Bacchus, Jupiter, Ceres, Juno, and Mercury.

Roman gods

Romans and Greeks believed in many of the same gods. In the following list, the Greek name follows the Roman name. Jupiter (Zeus) was god of the sky and king of all gods. His wife Juno (Hera) was goddess of women and mothers. All the gods were part of their family.

Mars (Ares) god of war; Ceres (Demeter) goddess of farming; Venus (Aphrodite) goddess of love and beauty; Minerva (Athena) goddess of crafts and wisdom; Mercury (Hermes) messenger of the gods; Diana (Artemis) goddess of the moon and hunting; Neptune (Poseidon) god of the sea; Vulcan (Hephaestus) god of the fire; Vesta (Hestia) goddess of the hearth; Bacchus (Dionysus) god of wine; Saturn (Kronos) god of farming; Janus, god of doorways and journeys; Apollo (Apollo) god of light and music.

TEMPLES AND SHRINES

Romans built **temples** as homes for their gods and goddesses. Inside each temple, there was a **shrine** with a statue of the god or goddess. Priests made sacrifices in front of these statues. On special days, Romans sacrificed animals outside the temples. It was important to get everything right, or the gods would be angry.

Priests looked for signs, or omens, from the gods. Thunder and lightning were bad omens. Romans never did anything if the omens were bad. People went to **augurs** and astrologers to find out the future. The services of augurs and astrologers were expensive, so poor people went to **soothsayers**.

This temple is in Nimes, France. Nimes was once part of the Roman Empire. These columns are copied from columns found in Greek temples.

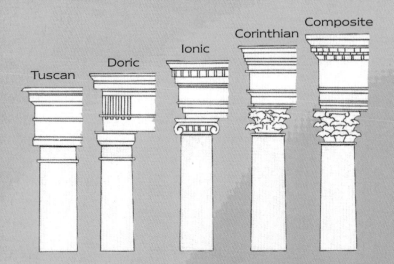

Tuscan   Doric   Ionic   Corinthian   Composite

The Romans used five types of column in their important buildings.

The Romans believed that the household gods helped them in their everyday lives. They believed the **lares** protected the home and the **penates** provided the family's food.

The Romans put small statues of the household gods in a shrine in front of the fire or in the courtyard of a house. People prayed to these gods when they woke up and when they left the house.

Medicine and healing

Romans thought illness was a punishment from the gods. They made sacrifices so the gods would cure an illness. The Romans began to learn about medicine from the Greeks. Archaeologists have found medical instruments like the ones in the picture. Stone carvings show doctors at work. Eye infections were a common problem. One carving shows an eye doctor treating a patient. Doctors sold ointments made from herbs. Pliny wrote about a mustard gargle that was good for upset stomachs. Roman doctors charged high prices, so poor people often went to a chemist first.

A ROMAN FARM

In early times, most Romans worked on their own small farms. During long years of war, the men were away fighting. Women and children struggled to keep the farms going. Some farms were given to army commanders as rewards for battle victories. Slaves worked their land. By about 100 BC nearly all farming was done on large estates.

The photograph is an aerial view of a large Roman farm at Estrees-sur-Noye in northern France. The drawing shows what archaeologists think the estate looked like in Roman times.

The *vilicus* lived in a smaller villa with small rooms for the slaves.

Some farm workers lived in slaves' quarters around the courtyard, near the cattle, pigs, and hens they looked after.

Storehouses

Gardens separate the main villa from the rest of the farm.

Some buildings in the courtyard would have been used as stables and cowsheds. One would have been a mill for grinding grain, and another a spinning and weaving room.

Main gate

Owners and managers

The owners of large farms were very wealthy. They lived in cities for most of the year. They only visited their farms in the summer, when it was too hot to be in the cities. Then, they stayed in a villa, which is a large house on the farm estate. A manager, called a vilicus, and a housekeeper, called the vilica, ran the farm. Slaves did the farm work.

Buildings and plants

Archaeologists have found Roman farm sites all over Europe and North Africa. From pieces of stone, brick, and tiles, they can tell what the buildings were like. From seeds and vegetable remains, they can tell which crops were grown.

In Italy, farmers grew vines, olives, and corn. Farms in Britain and France grew wheat, barley, beans, peas, plums, and apples. The Romans brought new crops, such as cabbages, carrots, cherries, and walnuts to Britain.

The big farms had gardens around the villa. The Romans planted hedges of yew, box, and cypress. They planted trees to give shade. They grew roses, lilies, and violets.

THE FARMING YEAR

Festivals

Each part of the farming year had a special festival. The Romans offered gifts to the gods before ploughing the land and sowing seeds. In May, every farm worker walked around the fields in a special procession asking the gods to help the crops ripen. In the fall, Romans celebrated the harvest with sports and feasts.

Running the farm

A farm estate was like a small town. It provided everything the farm workers needed. The vilicus and vilica were slaves. They had great responsibilities and worked hard.

Archaeologists found this mosaic in Carthage in North Africa. It was probably made in the 4th century AD. It shows a boar hunt. The Romans also hunted deer. They caught partridges, pheasants, and pigeons.

This mosaic shows slaves picking and pressing grapes to make wine. Romans grew enough grapes to make wine both for themselves and to sell to other countries.

Slaves made cheese from cow's and goat's milk. They looked after chickens, ducks, and geese. They collected honey from bees. They pressed olives for oil and ground grain into flour. They made woollen cloth.

Archaeologists found these Roman farm tools at Newstead on the Tweed River in Scotland. The scythe is made from iron. The rake on the right is made from the horns of a red deer.

The Roman calendar

Romans named some of their months after gods and goddesses: January (Janus), March (Mars), May (Maia), and June (Juno).
February came from the name of a special ceremony.
April meant "the opening of flowers".
Julius Caesar named July after himself and Augustus did the same with August.
Until 46 BC, the Roman year started on the first day of March.

A TOWN IN THE EMPIRE

Archaeologists have found Roman cities all over its vast empire. Some, such as Volubis in Algeria, are in ruins, but no one has built over them. Other Roman cities, such as Bath in England, have been built on for hundreds of years.

Beginnings

Some Roman towns began as forts where soldiers lived. Others began as new towns in conquered lands.

Thamugadi, now called Timgad in Algeria, North Africa, was built in AD 100 for Roman soldiers.

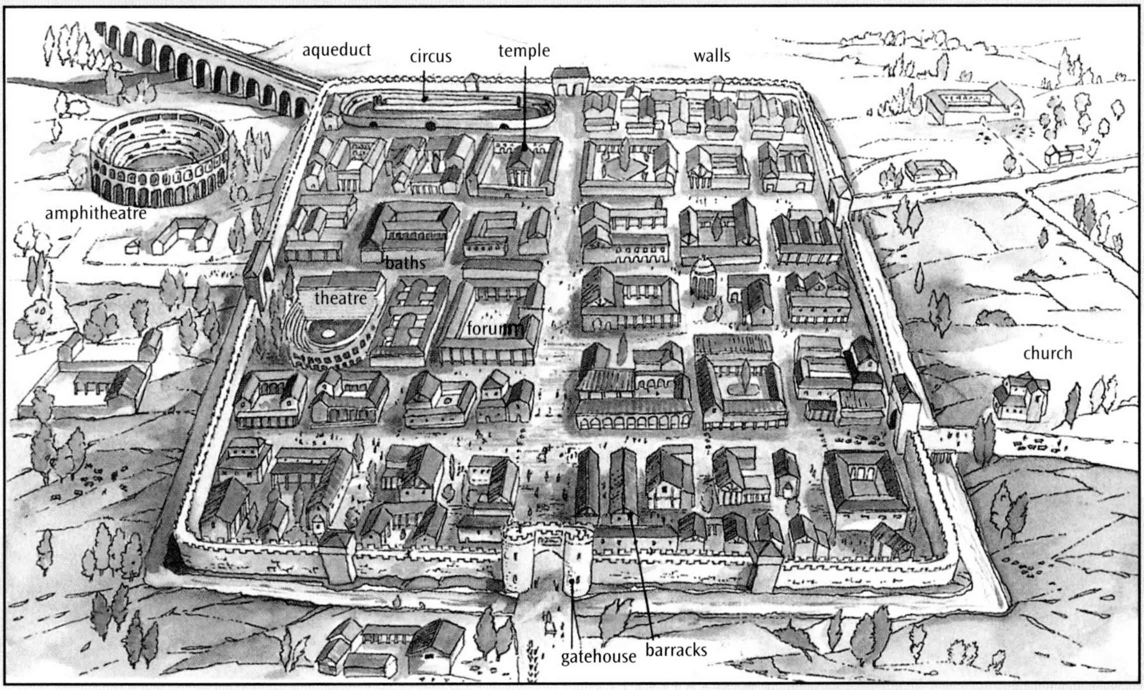
aqueduct
circus
temple
walls
amphitheatre
baths
theatre
forum
church
gatehouse
barracks

A Roman town

Town planning

Romans planned their cities on a grid system. The streets were straight and crossed each other at right angles. The roads divided the towns into squares.

Water

The Romans built **aqueducts** to carry water from lakes and rivers to their towns. Aqueducts carried water on a bridge across a valley or in pipes underground. Romans knew that clean water was important.

BUILDERS

Materials

Romans used stone and brick in their buildings. They invented a type of concrete in about 200 BC.

Arches

Romans used arches to hold up aqueducts, bridges, and tall buildings. They knew that squeezing an arch, which is a semicircle, against a central keystone is the strongest shape. It can carry the weight of a wall or hold up a roof.

These are carvings on Trajan's Column. It was built in AD 114 by the Emperor Trajan to celebrate a great victory. In the top row, soldiers are building stone fortifications. Fortifications were used to protect the soldiers during a battle.

Workers

Roman engineers, surveyors, and masons went all over the empire showing people how to build. The Romans used hundreds of slaves to build their projects.

Roman roads

The Romans built 85,000 kilometres (53,000 miles) of roads over their empire. Surveyors who travelled with the Roman army planned the roads. Surveyors worked out the most direct route. Then soldiers and slaves dug a wide trench along this route. They filled the trench with layers of sand, concrete, small stones, and stone blocks. Roman roads were very strong. The routes of Roman roads are still part of the road system in Britain and Europe.

This is a Roman aqueduct in Segovia, Spain. The two layers of arches carried water 36 metres (118 feet) above the streets. Romans looked for a lake or river that was higher than the town. Then, they built an aqueduct that sloped gently downhill to the town. They lined the water channel with concrete to keep the water from leaking.

INSIDE A TOWN HOUSE

Archaeologists dug in the volcanic ash and mud that covered Pompeii and Herculaneum. They found houses with furniture and pots and pans. From this, much is known about how the Romans lived in town houses.

Most town houses had central heating. Hot air from a furnace went through channels under the floor and through pipes in the walls. Some people had their own baths.

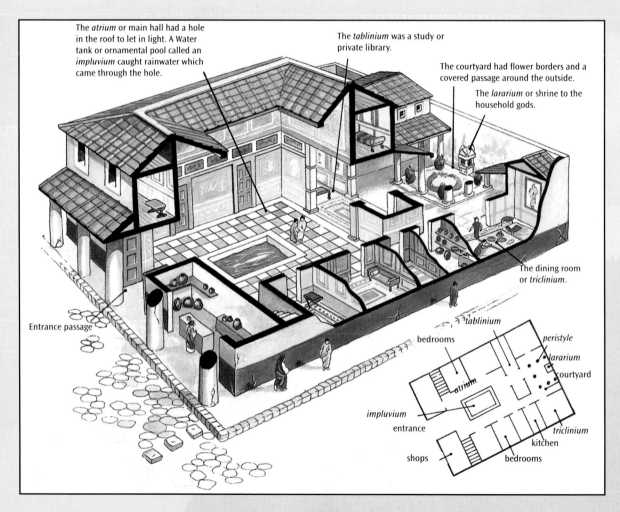

The *atrium* or main hall had a hole in the roof to let in light. A Water tank or ornamental pool called an *impluvium* caught rainwater which came through the hole.

The *tablinium* was a study or private library.

The courtyard had flower borders and a covered passage around the outside.

The *lararium* or shrine to the household gods.

The dining room or *triclinium*.

Entrance passage

tablinium
bedrooms
peristyle
lararium
courtyard
atrium
impluvium
entrance
triclinium
kitchen
shops
bedrooms

This street is in Herculaneum. Two families lived in these houses. One family lived on the upper floor, and the other family lived on the ground floor. In Rome, poorer people lived in flats. There were one-room schools and takeaway restaurants in the flats.

Furniture

Roman furniture was made from wood. Most of it has now rotted away. Wall paintings tell us something about what was in their homes.

Romans had beds, chairs, stools, and tables. They had wooden cupboards and chests in which they kept their books, clothes, and food. They had lamps that burned olive oil and candles made from reeds coated in wax.

Romans painted pictures on the walls of their houses. This one is in a house near Pompeii.

COOKING AND EATING

Early Romans ate very simply until they got new ideas about food from conquered lands. The first Romans did not bake bread. They ate boiled meat and a type of soup.

Mealtimes

Later Romans ate a breakfast of bread and cheese. Lunch was a cold meal of bread, meat, and fruit. The most important meal was dinner, which was eaten at about 4:00 in the afternoon. Roast meats, fish, fruit, and dessert were served. When there were guests, dinner lasted into the night.

A Roman kitchen might have looked like this. Wealthy people would have had slaves to cook food on charcoal stoves. Poor people cooked food in the streets or in a local baker's oven.

A feast

Romans lay on couches to eat. They ate with their fingers and with knives and spoons. Slaves served the meal and brought bowls of water and towels for people to wash their hands during a meal.

A feast had many courses. Romans ate shellfish, fish, wild boar, roast pheasant, partridge, peacocks, ostriches, fruit, and sweets. They drank wine, which they sometimes mixed with water or honey. Some of what we know about Roman food comes from a recipe book written by Marcus Apicius.

Between courses, the guests had serious conversations and discussions. There was usually some sort of musical entertainment. Slaves played musical instruments such as a type of harp called a **cithara.** They played panpipes and trumpets. Slave girls danced to the music.

Many Roman writers said that wealthy people ate too much and spent too much money on food. Pliny the Younger wrote that he went to feasts because he liked the conversation.

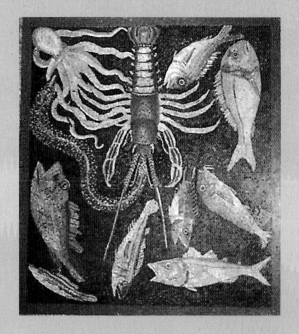

This mosaic shows the fish eaten by the Romans.

This mosaic was found in Cicero's villa at Pompeii. It shows street entertainers playing music and dancing.

AT THE BATHS

Wealthy people had baths in their own homes. Poorer people went to public baths in the town. They were not expensive, and in some towns, they were free. Most Romans enjoyed going to the baths. They relaxed there and chatted with friends.

There were more than 900 public baths in Rome. Men finished work at about 3:00 in the afternoon and then went to the baths. They would spend an hour there before going home for dinner. Women could only use the baths in the morning when the men were not there.

The Great Bath at Aquae Sulis is in western England. The town is now called Bath. This great bath was filled with water that flowed from a hot spring. People thought the water cured illnesses.

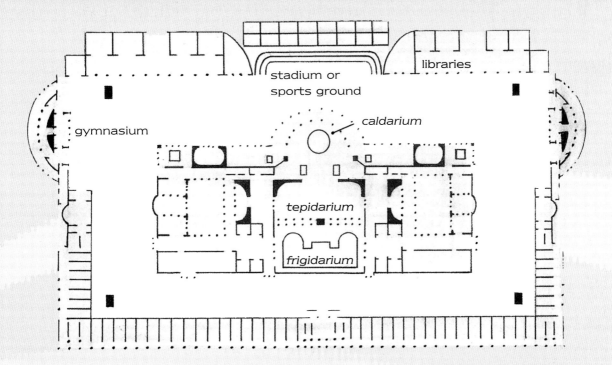

stadium or sports ground

libraries

gymnasium

caldarium

tepidarium

frigidarium

Bathing and exercise kept the Romans fit and healthy. First, a slave rubbed oil into the bather's body. Then, the bather went into the tepidarium where there were two baths of warm water. Next, the bather went into a very hot bath called a caldarium. The room was full of steam and made the bather sweat. The bather used a strigil to scrape oil and dirt off his or her skin, and then the bather plunged into a cold bath called a frigidarium. Finally, a slave rubbed scented oil into the bather's skin.

Several Roman baths still stand today. However, the large Caracalla Baths in Rome were destroyed by invading Goths 300 years after they were built. These baths, built between AD 206 and 235, could be used by 1,600 bathers at a time.

PUBLIC HOLIDAYS

The Romans did not have weekends off work, as most people do nowadays. Instead, they had 120 days of public holidays throughout the year. On these holidays, Romans watched plays or listened to concerts. They went to the amphitheatre to watch chariot races and gladiator fights.

Gladiators

Gladiators were slaves or criminals who were trained to fight. They fought each other or wild animals. They fought to the death in front of huge crowds.

Chariot races

Most towns had a special racetrack for chariot races. Hundreds of people came to watch. The Circus Maximus in Rome held 250,000 people.

Gladiators wore armour and a helmet. They fought with swords or three-pronged spears. This amphitheatre at El Djem, Tunisia, in Africa, had underground cages to hold wild animals that gladiators would fight.

Four teams of chariots raced against each other. Two or four horses pulled each chariot. Each team wore a different colour. The crowd cheered for their favourite team. Each race was seven laps of the circus, which was about 6.5 kilometres (4 miles).

At the theatre

Roman theatres were in the open air. People sat on stone seats arranged in a semi-circle around the stage. Some theatres held more than 7,000 people. The actors wore large masks because the audience was too far away to see their faces. Some masks were sad, and some were happy.

Chariot racing was very dangerous. The drivers bumped and rammed into each other. Chariots were often knocked over. The charioteers wore helmets and leather chest and leg protectors. Even so, they were sometimes hurt or killed.

CRAFTS AND CRAFTWORKERS

When Rome was a republic, the plebeians were craftworkers and tradesmen. By the end of the republic in 27 BC, wealthy landowners had slaves working their farms. These slaves took over the crafts from the plebeians. Many plebeian craftworkers moved to the towns.

City craftworkers

Craftworkers had their own workshops. They sold their goods from their workshops or in the local markets. Some craftworkers were helped by apprentices and slaves.

Goldsmiths, silversmiths, and jewellers made plates, goblets, and jewellery. Potters made clay pots, cups, and plates. Blacksmiths made tools, weapons, and pots and pans from iron. Carpenters carved furniture and farm tools from wood. Cobblers made boots and sandals. Leatherworkers made belts and shields for soldiers.

Raw materials

Craftworkers need raw materials with which to work. Jewellers imported emeralds and amethysts from India.

This wall painting of a potter's workshop is from Pompeii. Potters made tiles as well as pots. A workman scratched "I made 550 tiles" on a piece of Roman pottery. Another worker added "And I smashed 51." Both workers wrote in Latin.

Archaeologists have found Roman jars, bottles, bowls, and drinking glasses made from glass. Romans learned how to make glass from craftworkers in Syria. Glass objects like these were easy for a skilled craftworker to make.

Metalworkers got their gold and silver from Spain and Greece. Tin came from Britain. Copper came from Italy, Cyprus, and Spain. Miners worked underground. It was hot, dark, cramped, airless, and very dangerous.

SHOPS AND SHOPKEEPERS

Markets

Every city had a forum. This was the main market place as well as the place from where the city was governed. Rome had a big weekly market as well as smaller markets near the forum. These markets opened every day. They sold fruit, vegetables, meat, fish, and cloth.

Shops

The streets around the forum were crowded with shops. There were butchers, bakers, grocers, barbers, booksellers, and cloth sellers. At Pompeii, archaeologists have found shops with stone counters facing the street. Shops were run by families and worked by slaves.

Archaeologists have found many stone carvings of shops that show us what they looked like and what they sold. This is a carving of a butcher's shop. In wealthy families, slaves shopped for food. In other families, this job was usually done by men.

Buying and selling

Merchants and bankers had their offices in the forum. Merchants became rich by importing and exporting goods. They borrowed money from bankers to run their businesses. Bankers charged the merchants money for the loans. This was how bankers made their money.

Inspectors

Government inspectors visited markets and shops to check that food was accurately weighed and priced. They also checked for quality.

This coin is a bronze sestertius. It has the head of Emperor Nero on one side. Four sestertii were worth one silver denarii, and 25 denarii were worth one gold aureus.

This bakery was in Pompeii. Flour was ground in the mill on the right. The bakers lit a fire in the bottom part of the oven on the left. The bread was baked in the top part.

TRANSPORT

Coins and pottery

Archaeologists have found Roman coins in many different countries. This tells us that the Romans traded in countries far from Rome. Roman ships carried oil, flour, and wine in large pottery jars called **amphorae**. Archaeologists have matched bits of pottery they have found with workshops far away.

Wrecks

Archaeologists study wrecks of ships and their cargoes. They can tell where the ships came from and where they were going.

Trade in the empire

Ships

It was cheaper to carry goods by sea than overland. Roman ships had sails, and oars to use if there was no wind. Roman ships carried wheat, wine, silks, and spices. It took two to three weeks for a cargo ship to sail from Egypt to Rome.

Land travel

Some people preferred to travel by land. They were afraid of shipwrecks and pirates. Most Roman roads were safe, although there were some bandits. There were inns along main roads where travellers could stay over night. Government messengers changed their horses at these inns. They rode fast, carrying messages all over the empire. Ordinary people walked or rode donkeys and mules.

Archaeologists found this mosaic of ships and dolphins in Ostia. Ostia was a city at the mouth of the Tiber River. Large merchant ships anchored there. Then smaller ships took the goods to warehouses.

Transportation included animals pulling carts.

WAR WITH CARTHAGE

By 290 BC, the Romans were a strong force. They had defeated many of the people living on their borders. They had bribed other tribes to keep away.

War at sea

The Romans began to look for lands beyond their borders. This led to many years of war with the Carthaginians. These people came from the wealthy trading state of Carthage in North Africa. The Romans and the Carthaginians quarrelled over Sicily, an island in the Mediterranean Sea. They both wanted to control the island's ports and wheat fields. The Romans built a fleet of warships. They defeated the Carthaginians at sea in 241 BC.

Roman warships carried 400 soldiers. Roman ships attacked enemy ships by first ramming a huge spike into their sides. This fastened the ships together. Then Roman soldiers jumped on to the enemy ship and fought hand-to-hand.

War on land

The Carthaginian general Hannibal made a plan to attack Rome. He marched his army 1,900 kilometres (1,200 miles) and invaded Italy. The Carthaginians defeated a Roman army at Trebbia. A year later, they defeated the Romans at Lake Trasimene. Hannibal's army killed 70,000 Roman soldiers. Then his army marched south to Cannae, where again they defeated the Romans.

The Roman general, Scipio, decided to attack Carthaginian colonies. He conquered Spain in 207 BC and invaded North Africa. Hannibal rushed back to defend Carthage. At Zama, in 202 BC, Scipio defeated Hannibal's army. Hannibal escaped back to Carthage and made peace with Rome.

This coin has a portrait of Hannibal on one side and an elephant on the other. He was very young when he became a general, but even so, he nearly beat the Romans.

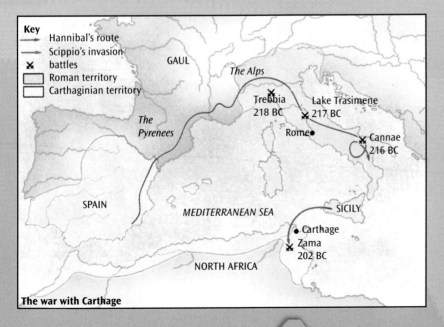

Key
→ Hannibal's route
→ Scippio's invasion
✗ battles
☐ Roman territory
☐ Carthaginian territory

GAUL

The Alps

The Pyrenees

Trebbia 218 BC

Lake Trasimene 217 BC

Rome

Cannae 216 BC

SPAIN

MEDITERRANEAN SEA

SICILY

Carthage
Zama 202 BC

NORTH AFRICA

The war with Carthage

Hannibal marched for five months with his army of 60,000 men and 37 elephants. It took 15 days to cross the Alps mountains on the way to Italy. Forty thousand men died.

LEGIONARIES AND CENTURIONS

The first Roman armies were made up of ordinary citizens. Young men were called up to fight a war. Older men cleaned weapons and defended their city. Then, in 107 BC, everything changed. Marius, who was a very clever general, became consul. He knew the army needed well-trained men who could fight. He planned a new army.

The Roman army

Men joined for 20 years as full-time soldiers. They were paid about 25 denarii a year, which was a good living. Roman soldiers were trained to march, fight, and build roads and bridges.

A standard bearer
Each legion had a standard. This was a pole with a silver eagle on the top and the legion's badges below. In battle, the standard was used to signal to the soldiers who were marching behind it.

A legionary
He wore an iron helmet and a metal cuirass to protect his body. His kilt was made from strips of leather and metal. He fought with a short sword, a dagger, and a long spear. He carried a leather shield.

The army was divided into **legions** of about 6,000 men. Each legion was made up of 10 **cohorts**. In each cohort, there were 6 centuries of about 100 men. Each legion also had a troop of about 700 cavalry. Legionaries were ordinary soldiers. A legionary could become a **centurion**, who commanded a century. A legate commanded a legion. Below him were six senior officers called tribunes.

By 27 BC, there were 28 legions. The soldiers lived in forts all over the empire.

Archaeologists have found Roman armour and weapons in Roman forts throughout the empire. Metal objects last a long time. They do not break into little pieces when buried underground.

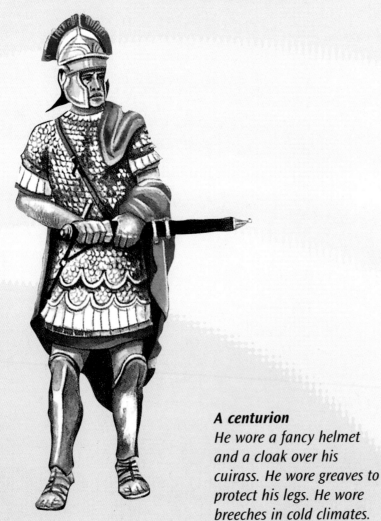

A centurion
He wore a fancy helmet and a cloak over his cuirass. He wore greaves to protect his legs. He wore breeches in cold climates.

WARFARE

Roman soldiers had to be strong. They had to carry all their own equipment when they marched. They also had to carry clothes, tents, food, and cooking pots. An army could march about 34 kilometres (21 miles) a day. Slaves went with the Roman army to help with the work.

Romans made many stone carvings of their battles. They made them on columns and arches that were built in memory of famous victories. The carvings on Emperor Trajan's column, built in AD 114, show details of Roman weapons, armour, and battle tactics.

This picture of Roman soldiers was made long after Roman times. The artist had studied Roman siege warfare.

Pontoon bridges

Roman armies crossed deep rivers on pontoon bridges. They made rafts of wood and tied them together. These rafts stretched from one bank to the other.

Camps

Each night the army set up camp. They dug a ditch and made earth walls to protect the camp from attack.

Siege warfare

The Romans pushed a moveable attack tower towards the enemy's walls. Soldiers on top of the tower hurled spears into the town. When the tower was close to the walls, a drawbridge was lowered. Then the soldiers swarmed across it into the town.

Defending a town

It was difficult to attack a strongly defended town. The town walls were made from thick stone and the doors from heavy wood. Soldiers stood on top of the town walls with spears to hurl and arrows to fire at the attackers. However, the Romans had ways of overcoming this and of laying siege to a defended town.

The Romans used a giant catapult called a ballista to hurl stones. Some catapults could throw stones weighing about 40 kilograms (88 pounds). This is a photograph of a ballista. It was built in modern times from a description written by Vitruvius, a Roman architect and engineer.

WARS IN ITALY

Quarrels between different groups
of people in Italy led to civil war.

Tiberius and Gaius

Wealthy men bought land and set up
farms that they worked with slaves.
Plebeians were forced off the land. In the
towns, there was no work for them. Then,
in 133 BC, Tiberius was elected tribune. He
had a plan to rent land to the plebeians,
but landowning Romans refused to give
up any of their land. Tiberius and 300 of
his supporters were murdered. Tiberius'
brother Gaius Gracchus was elected
tribune in 123 BC. He said the Senate
should buy wheat and sell it cheaply to
poor people. He said that all the people
should be Roman citizens, not just the
people of Rome. He was also murdered.

*The Romans were successful conquerors
because of their army. Pompey
brought great treasures back to Rome.*

Civil war

In 91 BC, the plebians rebelled. The Senate
sent two generals, Marius and Sulla, to
fight them. Many people died. In 90 BC,
the Senate promised to let all the people
be Roman citizens. Then Sulla and Marius
fought each other. The fighting went on
until 82 BC, when Sulla won control of
the Senate.

*The people supported Julius
Caesar because he was a
good general, like Pompey.*

The end of the republic

In 70 BC, Pompey, Sulla's brilliant and popular general, became a consul.

In 59 BC, Julius Caesar was elected consul. He became governor of southern Gaul, which is now France, and gradually brought northern Gaul under Roman rule. Pompey was jealous of Caesar. He got the Senate to order Caesar to resign his command. Caesar refused and marched into Rome with his army. Pompey fled to Greece where his army was defeated by Caesar's army. Pompey escaped to Egypt where he was murdered. Caesar returned to Rome in triumph. He ruled Rome as a dictator. Some senators hated this, and in 44 BC they murdered him.

Spartacus was an escaped slave. He led a revolt of 70,000 slaves. In 71 BC, Marcus Crassus led an army against the slaves. Spartacus was killed, and thousands of his supporters were crucified along the Appian Way. The story of Spartacus has been made into a ballet and a film. This is a photograph of a scene from the ballet.

THE EMPERORS

Octavian and Mark Antony

Octavian was Caesar's adopted son and heir. He and Mark Antony, a supporter of Caesar, tracked down Caesar's murderers. They killed the leaders, Cassius and Brutus. Then Octavian and Mark Antony divided the empire between them. Mark Antony ruled Egypt and the East. Octavian ruled Italy and the West.

Mark Antony fell in love with Cleopatra, the Queen of Egypt. Octavian was angry with Mark Antony for neglecting his empire, and they went to war. Their two war fleets met off the coast of Greece. Octavian's fleet won, and Mark Antony and Cleopatra killed themselves. Octavian returned to Rome in triumph. The Senate agreed that Octavian should become the first Roman emperor.

The Arch of Titus stands in the Forum in Rome. Titus was emperor from AD 79–81. He commanded the army that put down a Jewish revolt in Judea. The arch shows Roman soldiers carrying away Jewish treasure.

The Roman emperors

Augustus (27 BC–AD 14) did not try to gain new lands because he thought the empire was big enough. He chose the provincial governors and paid officials to help them. He built roads to link the provinces. He encouraged music and writing.

The next four emperors were all related to Augustus, but none of them ruled as well as he did.

Tiberius (AD 14–37) made the empire stronger, but became a tyrant later in his rule.

Emperor Augustus

Caligula (AD 37–41) carried on Tiberius' reign of terror and probably suffered from mental illness. He even made his horse a consul and built a special palace for it.

Claudius (AD 41–54) began the conquest of Britain.

Nero (AD 54–68) In AD 64, a great fire destroyed part of Rome. Nero blamed the Christians and had many of them killed. Eventually, his cruelty turned the people against him, and he killed himself.

After Nero, the emperor was usually a general. Under the reign of Trajan (AD 98–117), the empire reached its greatest size.

Augustus

Octavian changed his name to Augustus. He brought peace to the empire and made Rome a beautiful city. Augustus ruled as emperor until AD 14. Before he died, he chose his successor. Now the Roman people could not vote for their leader.

A ROMAN PROVINCE

Augustus took control of the whole empire. He set up a new system of governing the provinces. Each governor was in charge for three to five years. He was paid a salary and had officials to help him. He had to send reports back to Rome, collect taxes, and hear legal cases. Soldiers helped him keep control.

The conquest of Britain

Julius Caesar attempted to invade Britain in 55 BC. However, storms wrecked some of his ships, and his cavalry could not cross the sea to Britain. He tried again in 54 BC. This time he had 800 ships, 25,000 soldiers, and 2,000 cavalry. The Romans won battles against the local tribes. They made the conquered people send gifts to Rome.

Hadrian's Wall crossed Britain from east to west. It was 121 kilometres (75 miles) long, 6 metres (20 feet) high, and 3 metres (10 feet) wide. About 14,000 soldiers manned the wall. They lived in forts and kept watch from towers and gatehouses.

Archaeologists excavated a Roman palace at Fishbourne, in Sussex, England. This is one of the palace's mosaic floors.

Then Caesar and his army left. They were back in Rome before winter.

The Romans invaded Britain again in AD 43. Then Emperor Claudius conquered eastern and southern Britain. The British fought on in the north and west until their king, Caratacus, was defeated by the Romans in AD 51. In AD 78, Julius Agricola became governor of the province of Britannia, or Britain.

Life in Roman Britain

Britain became a more peaceful province of Rome. The Romans built temples, inns, and amphitheatres outside the walls of their forts. The soldiers defended the frontiers of the empire, such as Hadrian's Wall. Then, the workshops, hospitals, bath houses, and other fort buildings became part of the town that surrounded them.

The Romans taught the British people how to build homes from stone and towns with straight streets. Some Romans married British women. They and their children and grandchildren lived like Romans. They spoke Latin, had Roman furniture in their houses, and wore togas.

The Emperor Hadrian spent 15 years travelling around his empire. He ordered walls, ditches, and forts to be built to protect the borders of the empire from invaders. In Britain, he ordered a wall to be built from the Irish Sea to the North Sea. He wanted to stop tribes in Scotland from attacking the province.

THE FALL OF ROME

Tribes living outside the Roman Empire began attacking it. The Romans had to send more and more soldiers to defend the frontiers of their empire. Taxes had to be increased to pay for them. People did not want to pay higher taxes. There was unrest throughout the empire. The army split and supported the claims of different men to be emperor. Between AD 211 and 284, 20 emperors were murdered.

The government of the empire was in chaos. Then, in AD 410 and again in AD 476, the Goths, a Germanic tribe, invaded Italy and captured Rome. It was the end of the empire in the west. The Eastern Empire lasted until it was captured by the Turks in AD 1453.

In AD 284, the large Roman Empire was ruled by both Diocletian and Maximianus. Diocletian ruled the Eastern Empire, and Maximianus ruled the Western Empire. When they retired, civil war broke out.

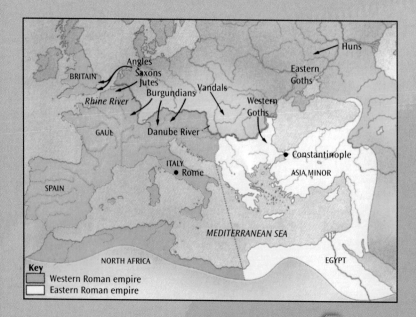

The Romans called all tribes outside their empire "barbarians". In AD 376, hordes of barbarians began invading the Roman Empire. Within 100 years, the "barbarians" ruled the Western Empire.

The legacy of Rome

The barbarian invaders destroyed many Roman towns and left them in ruins. People forgot the Roman ways.

However, Rome remained the centre of Christianity, and the Latin language was used in church services. It became the basis of most modern European languages and of government and law.

In the 15th century, a new age began. It was called the Renaissance, or rebirth. Scholars and artists rediscovered the architecture and writings of Rome and Greece. This rediscovery has inspired people ever since.

Today, the Pope is head of the Catholic Church and lives in Vatican City in Rome. After the fall of the empire, Rome remained the centre of the Christian Church. The Pope's priests spread Christianity throughout the barbarian tribes who had taken over the Western Empire. Latin remained the official language of the Church for hundreds of years.

TIMELINE

BC

753   The founding of Rome.

509   Tarquin the Proud, the last king of Rome, is driven out. Rome becomes a republic.

494   The plebeians are given the right to choose their own tribunes.

264   The First Punic War begins. Romans build their first warships and learn to fight at sea.

218   The Second Punic War begins. Hannibal marches across the Alps.

149   The Third Punic War begins. Carthage destroyed by the Romans. North Africa becomes a Roman province.

133   Tiberius becomes tribune of the people.

123   Gaius becomes tribune of the people.

107   Marius becomes consul and sets up a new army.

91   The plebeians rebel.

82   Sulla rules as a dictator.

73–1   Spartacus leads a slaves' revolt. Spartacus is killed and the slaves' revolt is defeated.

58–49   Julius Caesar conquers Gaul and invades Britain twice.

44   Julius Caesar is murdered.

43   Mark Antony and Octavian take power.

31   Battle of Actium: Octavian defeats Mark Antony.

27   Octavian becomes Augustus, the first emperor.

AD

14	Tiberius becomes emperor.
37	Caligula becomes emperor.
41	Claudius becomes emperor.
43	Claudius invades Britain.
64	A great fire destroys most of Rome.
79	Vesuvius erupts and destroys Pompeii and Herculaneum.
80	Emperor Titus opens the Colosseum in Rome.
114	Trajan's column is built in Rome.
122–126	Hadrian's Wall is built in northern England.
252	Barbarian tribes begin to invade the empire.
306	Constantine becomes emperor.
313	Christianity becomes the official religion of the Roman Empire.
395	The Roman Empire is divided into two halves.
410	The Germanic tribe of Goths attack Rome.
445	The Teutonic tribe of Vandals attack Rome.
476	The Western Empire is defeated by the Goths.
1453	The Eastern Empire is defeated by the Turks.

GLOSSARY

abacus wooden frame with rows of beads on wires used for counting

amphitheatre oval-shaped building with rows of seats around a central space where fights or games were held

amphora large, clay storage jar

apprentice someone who learns a trade by working with someone who is an expert

aqueduct sloping bridge or channel, often built on arches, for carrying water overland to towns

archaeologist person who finds out what happened in the past by excavating old buildings and objects

augur religious person

centurion leader of 100 soldiers

cithara small musical instrument

citizen person who lives in a city and helps to choose its rulers

clan group of related families that share an ancestor

cohort group of 600 men in the army

consuls two men elected for one year to be in charge of law and order in Rome

cremate to burn a dead body

druid priest of an old British religion

emperor ruler of an empire

empire group of countries under the rule of one country

excavate to dig in the ground to uncover buildings and objects

forum public meeting place

household gods gods that are special to one family

lares Roman household gods that protected the outside of the home

legion largest unit in the Roman army of 4,000 to 6,000 soldiers led by a legate

legionary foot soldier

magistrate person who makes laws and sees that they are carried out

mosaic pieces of glass, stone, or wood put together to form a picture or design

noble person born into an important family; the group of nobles in a country is called the nobility

patrician wealthy Roman citizen

penates Roman household gods that protected the inside of the home

philosopher person who studies the meaning of life

plebeian any Roman citizen who was not a patrician

priest man who performs all the duties and the ceremonies for worshipping the gods

province part of a country or empire ruled by a governor

republic country or group of countries where the people elect the government

sacrifice to kill an animal or person as an offering to the gods

Senate group of about 300 Romans who advised the magistrates

shrine holy place

soothsayer person who uses magic to predict future events

stola loose robe worn by women

stylus pointed tool used to write

temple building or place where people worship their god or gods

toga loose garment worn by Roman citizens

tribune man who represented the plebeians

underworld place where the spirits of the dead went

Further reading

You can find out more about the Ancient Romans in books and on the Internet. Use a search engine such as www.yahooligans.com to search for information. A search for the words "Ancient Rome" will bring back lots of results, but it may be difficult to find the information you want. Try refining your search to look for some of the people and ideas mentioned in this book, such as "Cicero" or "Roman gladiators."

More books to read

Ancient Rome, Jane Bingham (Hodder Wayland, 2006)

Encyclopedia of the Roman World (Usborne Publishing, 2004)

In the Daily Life of the Ancient Romans, Peter Hicks (Hodder Children's Books, 2003)

The Romans, R. Hull (Franklin Watts, 2004)

INDEX